_____

By

_____

On

_____

Dear Reader,

Jesus loves children!

One day, when some moms and dads brought their children to Jesus to receive a blessing, his disciples thought he was too busy. But he said, "Let the little children come to me." Jesus and the children talked and listened to each other and had a fun time together.

Jesus is now saying to you, "Come to me,

_____ (insert your name). Let's have some special times together."

Now that you've received your First Holy Communion, every Sunday can be a special time with Jesus.

Another special time with Jesus is when you go Confession, pray the Rosary, or say your morning and night prayers. Can you think of any other times? Maybe it's when you're with your family or friends. It can be any time, because Jesus is always with you.

This is your very own prayer book. You can read it at church or at home. I hope it will help you to have very special times with Jesus!

Angela Burrin

My First
Communion
Prayer Book

Traditional and New Prayers

Table of Contents

Prayers during My Day

Prayers at Mass

Prayers for Confession

Prayers with Mary

Prayer When I Wake Up

Jesus, thank you for this new day.
I want to please you in
everything I do.
I don't want to be so busy
that I forget you.
I know you won't forget me!
Jesus, whether I'm happy, sad,
excited, angry, worried,
or finding it hard to
forgive someone,
I know you will be with me
to guide me and help me.
Amen.

10

Psalm 118

This is the day that the Lord has made.

Let us rejoice and be glad today!

You are my God, and I will thank you.

You are my God,

and I will praise your greatness.

Thank the Lord because he is good.

His love continues forever.

The Sign of the Cross

In the name of the Father,
and of the Son,
and of the Holy Spirit.
Amen.

The Glory Be

Glory be to the Father,
and to the Son,
and to the Holy Spirit,
as it was in the beginning,
is now, and ever shall be
world without end.
Amen.

Prayer before Meals

Heavenly Father, great and good,
we thank you for this daily food.
Bless us even as we pray.
Guide and keep us through the day.
Amen.

Traditional Prayer before Meals

Bless us, O Lord, and these thy gifts
which we are about to receive
from thy bounty,
through Christ our Lord. Amen.

Prayer after Meals

We give you thanks,
Almighty God,
for these and all your gifts
which we have received
from your goodness,
through Christ our Lord.
Amen.

Prayer to My Guardian Angel

Angel of God,
my guardian dear,
to whom God's love
commits me here,
every day be at my side,
to light and guard,
to rule and guide.
Amen.

Prayer to the Holy Spirit

Holy Spirit, I'm happy that
when I was baptized
I received you into my heart.
Thank you for loving me just like
my heavenly Father and Jesus love me!
Holy Spirit, you know everything.
You are my special Helper.
Today, I need your help with
(tell the Holy Spirit).
Thank you for giving me
special graces whenever I ask!
Holy Spirit, I love you! Amen.

Come Holy Spirit

Come, Holy Spirit,
fill the hearts of your faithful.
And kindle in them the fire of your love.
Send forth your Spirit
and they shall be created.
And you shall renew
the face of the earth.

Prayer of St. Francis

Lord, make me an instrument of your
peace: where there is hatred, let me
sow love; where there is injury, pardon;
where there is doubt, faith; where there
is despair, hope; where there
is darkness, light; wnd where
there is sadness, joy.
O Divine Master, grant that I may
not so much seek to be consoled as
to console, to be understood as to
understand, to be loved as to love.
For it is in giving that we receive, it is
in pardoning that we are pardoned,
and it is in dying that we are
born to eternal life. Amen.

Psalm 23

The Lord is my shepherd. I have everything I need. He gives me rest in green pastures. He leads me to calm water. He gives me new strength. For the good of his name, he leads me on paths that are right. Even if I walk through a very dark valley, I will not be afraid because you are with me. Your rod and your shepherd's staff comfort me. You prepare a meal for me in front of my enemies. You pour oil of blessing on my head. You give me more than I can hold. Surely your goodness and love will be with me all my life. And I will live in the house of the Lord forever.

23

The Jesus Prayer

Lord Jesus Christ,

Son of God,

have mercy on me,

a sinner.

27

Prayer before a Crucifix

Look down upon me, good and
gentle Jesus, as before you I humbly
kneel. With all my heart,
I pray and ask you to put deep
within me faith, hope, love,
true sorrow for my sins, and a
desire to please you always.
Amen.

Jesus' Holy Cross

We adore you, O Christ,
and we bless you,
because by your holy cross
you have redeemed
the world.

Prayer When I Go to Bed

Thank you, Jesus,
for all the things I've done today.
I know you were with me all the time.
The most fun was (Tell Jesus).

I'm sorry, Jesus, for the things
I have thought, said, or done today
that didn't please you, like (Tell Jesus).

I pray, Jesus, for my family and friends
and other people too (Tell Jesus).

Jesus, it's the end of my day.

I know you'll be with me as I sleep.

Please give me happy dreams.

I love you, Jesus.

See you in the morning!

31

Prayer When I Arrive at Church

Hello Jesus, I'm here!

I can see the red light in the lamp

next to the Tabernacle, so I know you're there.

I'm sure you're happy to see me
because you said,
"Let the children come to me."
The Mass is about to begin.
I'll be praying, listening,
and singing too.
I'm so excited that I'll be
receiving you very soon
in Holy Communion.
When you are in my heart
I'll talk to you and you'll talk to me.
I love you, Jesus.
Amen.

The Confiteor

I confess to almighty God and to
you, my brothers and sisters, that I
have greatly sinned in my thoughts
and in my words, in what I have
done and in what I have failed to
do, through my fault, through my
fault, through my most grievous
fault; therefore I ask blessed Mary
ever-Virgin, all the Angels and
Saints, and you, my brothers and
sisters, to pray for me to the Lord
our God.

The Gloria

Glory to God in the highest, and on earth peace to people of good will. We praise you, we bless you, we adore you, we glorify you, we give you thanks for your great glory, Lord God, heavenly King, O God, almighty Father.

Lord Jesus Christ, Only Begotten Son, Lord God, Lamb of God, Son of the Father, you take away the sins of the world, have mercy on us; you take away the sins of the world, receive our prayer; you are seated at the right hand of the Father, have mercy on us.

For you alone are the Holy One, you alone are the Lord, you alone are the Most High, Jesus Christ, with the Holy Spirit, in the glory of God the Father.
Amen.

The Nicene Creed

I believe in **one God**, the Father almighty, maker of heaven and earth, of all things visible and invisible.

I believe in **one Lord Jesus Christ**, the Only Begotten Son of God, born of the Father before all ages. God from God, Light from Light, true God from true God, begotten, not made, consubstantial with the Father; through him all things were made. For us men and for our salvation he came down from heaven, and by the Holy Spirit was incarnate of the Virgin Mary, and became man.

For our sake he was crucified under Pontius Pilate, he suffered death and was buried, and rose again on the third day in accordance with the Scriptures. He ascended into heaven and is seated at the right hand of the Father. He will come again in glory to judge the living and the dead and his kingdom will have no end.

I believe in **the Holy Spirit**, the Lord, the giver of life, who proceeds from the Father and the Son, who with the Father and the Son is adored and glorified, who has spoken through the prophets.

I believe in **one, holy, catholic and apostolic Church**. I confess one Baptism for the forgiveness of sins and I look forward to the resurrection of the dead and the life of the world to come. Amen.

The Sanctus

Holy, Holy, Holy Lord
God of hosts. Heaven and
earth are full of your glory.
Hosanna in the highest.
Blessed is he who comes
in the name of the Lord.
Hosanna in the highest.

The Memorial Acclamation

We proclaim your Death, O Lord,
and profess your Resurrection
until you come again.

or

When we eat this Bread and
drink this Cup,
we proclaim your Death, O Lord,
until you come again.

or

Save us, Savior of the world,
for by your Cross and Resurrection
you have set us free.

The Our Father

Our Father, who art in heaven,
hallowed be thy name.
Thy kingdom come.
Thy will be done on earth,
as it is in heaven.
Give us this day our daily bread,
and forgive us our trespasses,
as we forgive those who trespass
against us, and lead us not
into temptation,
but deliver us from evil.
Amen.

The Lamb
of God

Lamb of God, you take away
the sins of the world, have
mercy on us. Lamb of God,
you take away the sins of the
world, have mercy on us.
Lamb of God, you take away
the sins of the world,
grant us peace.

Lord,
I Am Not Worthy

Lord, I am not worthy that
you should enter under my
roof, but only say the word
and my soul shall be healed.

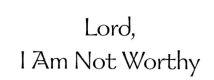

49

Prayer before Communion

Jesus, it's almost time for me
to receive you in the Eucharist.
I'm so glad that
I'm old enough now!
Jesus, this is our special
time together.
I believe that it is really you that
I am about to receive.
Jesus, it's time for me to
leave my seat
and to walk up the aisle.
Let me say, "Jesus, I
love you" all the way!

Prayer after Communion

Jesus, you are really present
in the Eucharist.
Thank you for coming
into my heart.
You are holy, awesome,
powerful, and kind.
Thank you for my life,
my family, my friends,
and the priest who said Mass.
Jesus, what do you want
to say to me?
(Take some time to listen.)
Amen.

St. Michael the Archangel

St. Michael the Archangel,

defend us in battle,

be our protection against the

wickedness and snares of the devil.

May God rebuke him, we humbly pray,

and do thou,

O Prince of the heavenly host,

by the power of God,

cast into hell Satan

and all the evil spirits

who prowl about the world

seeking the ruin of souls.

Amen.

Prayer before Confession

Jesus, I'm going to meet you in Confession!

I know the priest is taking your place.

Jesus, I want to be honest and tell the priest
what I've done wrong.

Please, Holy Spirit, help me to remember
what I need to confess.

Jesus thank you for dying on the cross
for all of my sins.

I can't wait for the priest to say,

"I absolve you from your sins in the
name of the Father, and of the Son,
and of the Holy Spirit."
Jesus, I'm so happy that
my sins will be forgiven and
forgotten!
Amen.

An Act of Contrition

My God, I am sorry for my sins
with all my heart.
In choosing to do wrong
and failing to do good,
I have sinned against you
whom I should love above all things.
I firmly intend, with your help,
to do penance,
to sin no more,
and to avoid whatever
leads me to sin.
Amen.

60

Help Me to Forgive

Jesus, I'm feeling hurt,
and I'm finding it hard to forgive.
You know what it's like to be hurt,
and you always forgave.
Holy Spirit, help me to forgive.
I know I don't have to feel like it
and that forgiving is a decision.
Give me the strength I need.
Father, thank you for loving me
and forgiving my sins.
I choose now to forgive
(name them).
I hope I can tell them soon,
"I forgive you." Amen.

You Said Yes!

When you were a young woman
living in Nazareth,
an angel visited you and asked you
to become the mother of Jesus.
You must have been so surprised.

Mary, I'm so glad that you said yes!
Now you are my mother too.

So I ask you to watch over me
and pray for me always.
I know that I can count on you
to bring my prayers for
(name them) to your Son, Jesus.
Thank you for your love and care.
Amen.

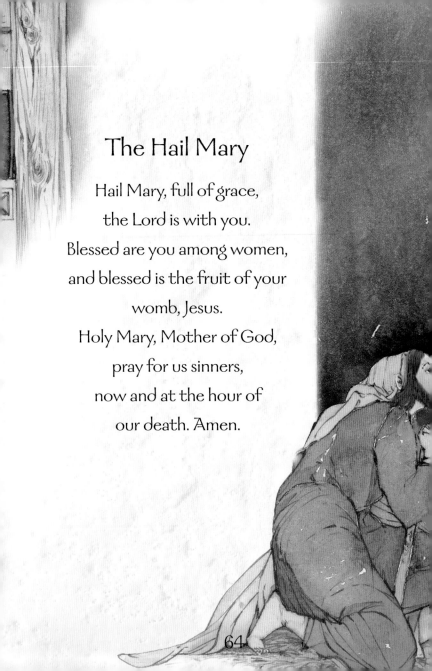

The Hail Mary

Hail Mary, full of grace,
the Lord is with you.
Blessed are you among women,
and blessed is the fruit of your
womb, Jesus.
Holy Mary, Mother of God,
pray for us sinners,
now and at the hour of
our death. Amen.

65

The Hail Holy Queen

Hail, holy Queen, Mother of mercy,
our life, our sweetness, and our hope.
To you do we cry, poor banished children of Eve;
to you do we send up our sighs,
mourning and weeping in this valley of tears.
Turn, then, most gracious advocate,
your eyes of mercy toward us;
and after this, our exile,
show unto us the blessed fruit
of your womb, Jesus.
O clement, O loving, O sweet Virgin Mary.
Pray for us, O Holy Mother of God,
that we may be made worthy of
the promises of Christ.

The Angelus

The angel of the Lord declared unto Mary:
And she conceived of the Holy Spirit.
Hail Mary . . .

Behold the handmaid of the Lord:
Be it done unto me
according to your word.
Hail Mary . . .

And the Word was made flesh:
And dwelt among us.
Hail Mary . . .

Pray for us, O holy Mother of God,
that we may be made worthy of the
promises of Christ.

The Joyful Mysteries of the Rosary

Prayed on Mondays and Saturdays

1. **The Annunciation** (Luke 1:26-38)
The angel Gabriel tells Mary that
she will have a son named Jesus.

2. **The Visitation** (Luke 1:39-56)
Mary visits her cousin Elizabeth.
Elizabeth's son will be John the Baptist.

3. **The Birth of Jesus** (Luke 2:1-19;
Matthew 1:18-2:12)
Jesus is born in a stable in Bethlehem.
Shepherds and kings visit him.

4. **The Presentation** (Luke 2:22-40)
Mary and Joseph take Jesus to
the Temple to present him to God.

5. **Finding of Jesus in the Temple**
(Luke 2:41-52)
After three days, Mary and Joseph
find Jesus teaching in the Temple.

The Luminous Mysteries
of the Rosary

Prayed on Thursdays

1. **The Baptism of Jesus** (Matthew 3:13-17)
Jesus is baptized by his cousin John
in the River Jordan.

2. **The Wedding Feast at Cana** (John 2:1-11)
Jesus changes the water into wine.
Mary was there!

3. **Jesus Proclaims the Kingdom of God**
(Mark 1:14-20)
Jesus tells the crowds about God's love and
performs miracles.

4. **The Transfiguration** (Luke 9:28-36)
Jesus shines like light. God says, "This is my Son.
He is the One I have chosen."

5. **The Institution of the Eucharist**
(Mark 14:22-25)
Jesus takes bread and says,
"Take it. This bread is my body."

74

The Sorrowful Mysteries of the Rosary

Prayed on Tuesdays and Fridays

1. The Agony in the Garden
(Luke 22:39-46)
Jesus prays for strength
to suffer and die for us.

2. The Scourging (John 19:1-3)
Jesus is tied to a pillar
and cruelly beaten by soldiers.

3. The Crowning with Thorns
(Matthew 27:27-31)
Soldiers put a circle of thorns
on Jesus' head.

4. The Carrying of the Cross
(Matthew 27:32)
Jesus falls three times.

5. The Crucifixion (Matthew 27:35-50)
Jesus dies on the cross.

The Glorious Mysteries of the Rosary

Prayed on Wednesdays and Sundays

1. The Resurrection
(Matthew 28:1-10)
Jesus rises from the dead.

2. The Ascension
(Luke 24:44-53)
Jesus returns to heaven.

3. The Coming of the Holy Spirit
(Acts 2:1-12)
Jesus sends his Holy Spirit
to the disciples.

4. The Assumption of Mary
Mary is taken up into heaven.

5. The Crowning of Mary
(Revelation 12:1)

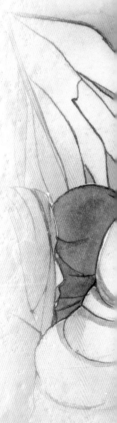

List of Biblical Illustrations